PULBROOK & GOULD

flowers

PULBROOK & GOULD
flowers

SONJA WAITES

with SHARON AMOS

photography by DAVID MONTGOMERY

COLLINS & BROWN

First published in Great Britain in 1999
by Collins & Brown Limited
London House
Great Eastern Wharf
Parkgate Road
London SW11 4NQ

1 3 5 7 9 8 6 4 2

British Library Cataloguing-in-Publication Data:
A catalogue record for this book
is available from the British Library.

ISBN 1 85585 707 3

Conceived, edited and designed by Collins & Brown Limited

Editor: Gillian Haslam
Copy Editor: Alison Wormleighton
Designer: Christine Wood

Reproduction by Hong Kong Graphic and Printing Ltd
Manufactured in China for Imago

Pulbrook & Gould Limited
Liscartan House
127 Sloane Street
London SW1X 9AS
Telephone: 0171 730 0030
Fax: 0171 730 0722
Website: www.pulbrook&gould.com

contents

foreword

I've loved flowers since I was a young girl playing in my mother's garden, but I first became aware that there was a relationship between glamour and flowers in my teens and early twenties. It was that early 1970s' moment when we were spellbound by the heroines of the 1930s' movies – all those blonde divas in their bias cut satin gowns who were somehow always surrounded by gorgeous bouquets of lilies. It was much later that my interest in flowers became more serious, in a business sense. When I became editor of British *Vogue* in 1987, I realized that the ability to send the right flowers to the right person on the right occasion was an essential part of running my office. In the fashion industry people give and receive flowers constantly, and probably no sector is more finely tuned to the nuances of meaning and minutely changing shades of taste that are conveyed in a bunch of flowers. More than anything, when you are moving in those circles, you quickly come to understand the difference between flowers that have been chosen with love and attention and those that haven't.

That's where Pulbrook & Gould came into my life. During my years at *Vogue* we developed a great relationship whereby I knew, with absolute certainty, that I could call up and have my ideas understood, interpreted and regularly surpassed by their talented team. It wasn't simply that I came to trust Pulbrook & Gould as a perfect representative in terms of style (what they create is always breath-taking) but, as I soon discovered, the depth of their experience and the breadth of their knowledge of people meant I could put myself completely in their hands. they would sort out any dilemma I had. When I wanted to send flowers to the Duchess of York for a dinner, without being quite sure what she likes, someone at Pulbrook & Gould would assure me, 'Oh, she loves those tiny white roses!' And when it came to the even steeper challenge of flowers for the Princess of Wales – what then? How to choose something outstanding for the woman to whom most of London was sending flowers? How to make it personal? How to be sure you weren't duplicating somebody else's gift? Somehow Pulbrook & Gould, armed with their extraordinary taste and insider knowledge, always had the most inspiring solution up their sleeves. Our creative relationship has continued even since I moved to New York in the early 1990s to edit *Harper's Bazaar*; and so I am delighted to be reminded of all those happy London days by the glorious work in this book.

Liz Tilberis
1947-1999

THATCHED HOUSE LODGE
RICHMOND PARK
SURREY
TW10 5HP

22nd February, 1999

Dear Lady Pulbrook –

Pulbrook & Gould have played a very important part in my life, starting with my wedding and on many other happy occasions.

The wonderful flower arrangements created by them have given enormous pleasure to myself and countless others.

Long may Pulbrook & Gould continue its outstanding success in the floristry world.

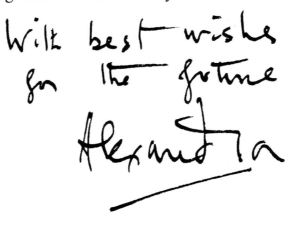

With best wishes
for the future

Alexandra

introduction

When Susan Pulbrook and Rosamund Gould first joined forces, they could little have suspected how their partnership would completely transform the way we buy and display flowers today. This book looks at their visionary use of flowers – the way they brought humble garden flowers to the table and made it their aim to bring the country right into the heart of the city.

The first chapter, *The Vision*, sets the scene, charting the beginnings of Pulbrook & Gould and describing some of their major achievements and unrivalled successes. It reveals how the social climate has a surprising and profound effect on the cut-flower market, while giving an intriguing glimpse behind the scenes into the everyday running of their shop.

Classic Visions introduces Pulbrook & Gould's timeless grand style, with the creation of magnificent flowers for dinner parties, soirées and society weddings, plus a series of smaller arrangements that perfectly illustrate the way flowers can be used in the widest variety of occasions.

Contemporary Visions brings us right up to date, introducing flowers for uncluttered open-plan spaces and demonstrating the very cutting edge of floral design that is almost sculptural in its origins. The influence of flower colour on a room is described, as is the choice of flowers to suit a particular style of architecture.

Country Visions returns to Pulbrook & Gould's roots, showing the simple charm of hedgerow flowers and garden plants at their humblest – informal armfuls of the most gorgeous, quintessentially English flowers.

Finally, the tools of the trade, and also some of the tricks, that Pulbrook & Gould make particular use of, from tying posies and lining containers to making circlets of flowers and malmaison roses, are revealed in the final chapter, *The Workshop*.

We hope you will enjoy this visit to one of the most respected florists of our time and the chance to feast your eyes on the glorious photographs of some of their most ravishing arrangements.

the vision

the vision

When Lady Pulbrook and Rosamund Gould set up in business in 1956, it was their flair

for turning the art of flower arranging on its head that set them apart from the rest of

the floristry world. They dared to put the humblest garden flowers on the grandest

tables, perplexing guests who wondered just what these unfamiliar blooms could be.

The flowers, in fact, were more than likely to have been growing under their noses in

their own gardens – but no one had ever thought to bring them indoors before.

Rosamund Gould had trained under Constance Spry, the renowned flower arranger

who began the vogue for a natural, 'loose' look. Susan Pulbrook was seeking a

diversion that might in some way help her come to terms with the death of her

husband, Sir Eustace. (He had been chairman of Lloyd's, was knighted in 1943 and

was awarded the Lloyd's Gold Medal for distinguished services.)

Above: A detail of tulips in pristine white and yellow. Opposite: Fresh from the grower in Cornwall, a newly opened crate of Christmas roses (*Helleborus niger*) in perfect condition. Although they are hardy garden plants, Christmas roses for the cut-flower trade are grown under glass to protect the flowers from the weather. Wooden battens hold the delicate heads carefully in place on the journey to London.

They took a lease on a small shop on Sloane Street, in London's Knightsbridge, and they were in business. Lady Pulbrook's butler was not amused and his comment on her early-morning trips to Covent Garden market has passed into legend. 'If her ladyship has to go into trade,' he stated, 'I don't know why she can't open a hat shop – no lady buys a hat before ten in the morning.'

But she persisted and Pulbrook & Gould became known for their trademark – that of bringing country flowers to the city. Time and again they forced people to take a second look at what was naturally available, breaking down the barriers between flowers hitherto considered suitable for indoor arrangements and those grown in the garden or growing wild in the hedgerows. Their flowers successfully create an illusion that the host has simply slipped out to the herbaceous border, scissors in hand, and returned bearing a bunch of flowers with the morning dew still on them.

Together they formed a formidable partnership and business bloomed. By the mid-1960s, Pulbrook & Gould ran a team of sixteen 'decorators', as the florists were referred to, who went all over the country turning homes and marquees into flights of flowering fancy for every occasion: debutante balls, weddings, parties for Ascot and the Derby. By this time they were working from three separate buildings in Sloane Street and running a fleet of eight vehicles, whose management alone was a full-time job.

Below left and below right: Pulbrook & Gould's large arrangements are impossible to transport successfully and so staff have to work in situ at the venue. The flowers are usually arranged the day before to avoid clashing with, for example, caterers, then there is a final check on the day itself. Besides the flowers, essential tools for the job are wire netting, sharp scissors and a panoply of tapes and fine wires.

They became the florists to whom everyone in the know, including royalty, automatically turned. For the Duke and Duchess of Kent's wedding, in 1961, York Minster was transformed with thousands of white roses; when Princess Alexandra was married in 1963, Pulbrook & Gould filled London's St James's Palace with pink camellias. In their initial foray into wedding flowers, however, Lady Pulbrook uncovered a floral monopoly among London's top churches. She was asked by the bride's mother to decorate a certain church, but the vicar intervened, saying that she could not do so because she was not 'on his list'. The ensuing debate hit the headlines back in the late 1950s and the 'list' certainly didn't last long after that.

Regular visitors to the shop included Lady Diana Cooper, the celebrated actress, who would pull up in her Mini and swan into the shop in a big straw hat for a bunch of her favourite flowers. Dilettante and art collector Bunny Roger was passionate about flowers and always wore a Pulbrook & Gould buttonhole; he also commissioned Pulbrook and Gould to do the flowers and themes for his many parties, including tenting the ceiling with navy blue silk and studding it with tiny lights to resemble the night sky.

On such occasions, their imagination has never been restrained by circumstance or cost. Typically, at one Ascot party for John Aspinall in the 1960s, a country house was turned into a nightclub by panelling the walls with hand-made box topiary shaped into

Smaller flower arrangements can be made up in the shop for collection by the customer, who will often have brought in a favourite container to be filled, as well as supplying details of the room the arrangements are destined for, its colour scheme and, of course, the occasion.

And sometimes, in a branch of blossom,
Or a lily deep,
An elf comes, plucked with the flower
In her sleep.

Mary Webb, *The Elf*

arches and columns; urns filled with white stocks stood in every alcove, and illusory fountains wrought from sprays of carnations sprang from antique epergnes. For a coming-out party, the ground floor of London's Dorchester Hotel was transformed – just for one night – into a country garden with banks of herbaceous borders, a real fountain with real fish, plus fragments of antique stone and statuary. Yet another dance featured a marquee hung with deep blue silk and swathes of purest white jasmine and stephanotis that looked and smelt divine. Panels of fruit and vegetables cleverly worked into pictures depicting the four seasons were created for one special party. For a wedding reception at London's Savoy Hotel, they decided to enclose the cake table with a clipped box hedge and miniature picket fence – the hedge was assembled from shaped wire netting completely covered in hundreds of short stems of box, which were then sheared into shape, making it indistinguishable from the real thing.

Rarely is such style seen now. Change in the cut-flower business began in the 1970s as a direct reflection of world events and economies. The lowering of the voting age rendered coming-out parties irrelevant and the oil boom altered the whole pattern of society. The oil barons who flocked to London gave parties and entertained with quite a different view on how flowers should be used. The same boom that gave them the freedom to entertain on a lavish scale brought crisis to many small growers. As fuel costs soared, it was no longer cost-effective to grow flowers in heated greenhouses, and so availability changed – the gardenia all but disappeared as a cut flower as it became uneconomical to heat greenhouses for bushes that would yield only three flowers each a day.

British growers are all-important to Pulbrook & Gould and always have been. When Susan Pulbrook and Rosamund Gould first began using cow parsley (similar to Queen Anne's lace in the US) and lady's mantle in arrangements, they had to raid their own gardens for supplies. As demand grew, Lady Pulbrook was obliged to call on private gardeners and estates to help her out. These days, both flowers are established species on the cut-flower market. Scabious and phlox, which everyone is using today, had to come from a selection of gardens that Lady Pulbrook had good relations with.

The Pulbrook & Gould shop is filled with light, plus colour and fragrance from hundreds of flowers. In the foreground is a basket of dried lavender with a miniature orange tree behind, while on the table a pot of *Phalaenopsis* stands next to violet-blue anemones and delphiniums. Lichen moss topiaries on the floor represent the cutting edge of modern floral arrangements, while in the background is a mass of cow parsley – one of Lady Pulbrook's signature flowers.

And frosts are slain and flowers begotten,
And in green underwood and cover
Blossom by blossom the spring begins.

A E Swinburne, *Atalanta in Calydon*

They revolutionized the market for foliage in a similar way. When they began in business, background foliage was severely limited – just greeny-grey eucalyptus and asparagus fern. Now, thanks to their persistence, you are just as likely to find a bouquet with fennel, great spiny artichoke leaves or silvery whitebeam, all garden choices that would once never have made it into a sophisticated flower arrangement.

Today's growers are mainly based in Cornwall and Devon, in the south-west of England, where the relatively milder climate gives them an edge in producing flowers slightly ahead of time. From the greenhouses of these two counties come boxes of Christmas roses (wrapped in tissue and packed between wooden battens to stop the nodding flower heads from moving in transit), crates of lily of the valley and posies of the first snowdrops.

Early-morning deliveries have to be sorted into flowers for specific orders and cut flowers for the shop. In the foreground is a bucket of greeny-yellow bupleurum, standing next to trays of cyclamen in perfect condition. The table is piled high with ranunculus and anemones.

At Pulbrook & Gould the seasons rule: daffodils in September and delphiniums in January are frowned upon. The earliest lilies of the valley cause much excitement when they arrive in the shop, even though their appearance is as predictable – or not – as the weather. Every flower has its season and none is scorned. The much-maligned carnation is invaluable in its native month of July, when it stands up to heat and drought; the same is true of gladioli; while garden chrysanthemums are wonderful in autumn, providing a welcome splash of colour and earthy scent. Mass marketing has had a detrimental effect on these flowers. By being perpetually on sale, at supermarkets and street stalls, they have become devalued. Now nobody wants them – they are merely bought as a stopgap until something better comes into flower.

Fashions in flowers come and go, and flowers are also inextricably linked to the fashion industry itself. As colours from the catwalk find their way into the home as shades of paint, vibrant cushions and throws, so toning flowers are in demand to continue interior decorating themes. Colour is strongly seasonal too, with pastels predominating in summer and strong colours in autumn as the year draws to a close. White and cream are available all year round – classic shades in both fashion and flower arranging.

Above: Benches are strewn with the raw materials for table arrangements, for filling vases and for typical country bunches. Opposite: Hammering tough stems of foliage with a wooden mallet improves water uptake and stops the flowers from wilting.

...those lilies, more imperious than orange blossom, more passionate than the tuberose, which climb up the staircase at midnight and come to find us in the very depth of our slumbers.

Colette

It's not unreasonable to compare Pulbrook & Gould to a firm of couturiers. The flower arrangements are labour-intensive and expensive, just like haute couture clothes, but like many a grand fashion house, they also have a diffusion range – a cheaper range of goods that give customers a taste of the real thing on a smaller scale. In Pulbrook & Gould's case, the company has diversified into garden beauty products – balms and lotions to soothe hands roughened by spadework and pruning. There is also the Pulbrook & Gould school, where courses are run to initiate novices into the arcane secrets of flowers and flower arranging.

Not only did Pulbrook and Gould change the way we look at flowers, but they also had a powerful influence on the etiquette of giving them. They instilled the custom of sending flowers before dinner so that they can be magnificently in place when guests arrive, to avoid adding to a busy host's workload by turning up flowers in hand.

The mechanics of the business have changed little since the early days. A buyer still has to rise with the lark and head for London's Covent Garden flower market every day with a list of orders from the shop. She has to use her expertise to decide whether the flowers are right for buying for a function days ahead: the flowers have to be properly conditioned so that, on the day, every bud is open yet not so overblown that petals will drop in a gust of warm air. The buyer also has licence to buy on impulse, if something irresistibly stunning is on offer. Then there are the daily deliveries from private growers, sometimes with flowers plunged in buckets of water in summer when the temperatures rise. Once the flowers arrive in the shop, it's a fine balance to maintain the temperature so that tender orchids don't catch a chill and yet lilies aren't persuaded to open fully before they are needed.

A posy of anemones, nerines, roses and mixed garden foliage including berried ivy, tied with raffia or rustic twine, is just the right size to be held in the hand.

At tables in the cool and moss-damp basement, nimble-fingered staff are at work at benches. They might be combining jasmine and roses into a bridal 'shower', a sort of trailing, elongated posy. Or they could be 'pipping' flowers, that is, splitting them into their constituent florets, and then carefully wiring each tiny piece with fine silver wire so that they can be bound into the lightest and prettiest bridesmaid's headdress. There are piles of rustic baskets waiting to be filled with primroses and delicate woodland cyclamen in season, heaps of wire netting and bundles of raffia – the tools of the trade – ready to work their magic. Two enormous fridges keep made-up arrangements – circlets, bridal posies, table arrangements – in perfect condition until they are needed.

At Covent Garden today there are flowers flown in from all around the world: orchids from Singapore, banksias from Australia, proteas from South Africa, roses and tuberoses from Kenya and carnations from Colombia. In the midst of such temptation Pulbrook & Gould are resolute about sticking to seasonal, British-grown flowers. You will find exotic orchids like Phalaenopsis in the shop, but they are grown under glass in Britain.

Selecting flowers from the shop for a natural country arrangement using familiar garden flowers and foliage, such as abelia and spray roses.

Phalaenopsis is fast becoming the azalea of our times, the most popular pot plant to give and to receive: beautiful and exotic, it is also considerably longer-lasting and easier to care for than somewhat temperamental azaleas. They fit perfectly into more contemporary homes, where their strong, open shapes hold their own in vast open-plan lofts and converted warehouses.

Their availability is a direct result of advances in technology. Cloning techniques have made orchids into viable commercial plants by reducing the time span from tiny plant to

Tying in stems of *Phalaenopsis* flowers with dogwood sticks is not only a practical way to support the flowers but also a means of highlighting their upright linear appearance.

flowering specimen from seven years to fewer than three. Similarly, new methods for drying and preserving plant materials have made possible exciting and avant-garde topiary arrangements.

As technology moves on, so does the commercial world. When rents and rates began to spiral in the 1980s, the cost of running three separate premises proved untenable and Pulbrook & Gould were forced to look for new premises. Moving into the modern surroundings of Liscartan House – still on Sloane Street – was a catalyst for the company

Revolutionary growing techniques have made orchids affordable pot plants, and their tolerance of heated rooms and unfussy watering regimes has made them justifiably popular.

to rethink the business, to streamline it in keeping with the contemporary shell of the building while still retaining their classic stamp.

Some years before the move, Rosamund Gould married and decided that the time was right for her to 'retire' to the country. At this point, in 1976, Sonja Waites, Lady Pulbrook's sister-in-law, came to the fore. She had helped out at the shop in the 1960s and caught the tail end of the grand era of deb dances and elaborate marquees, before witnessing the great changes the business went through. And so she is ideally placed to help guide Pulbrook & Gould into the next century.

To adapt to new styles of living, Pulbrook & Gould have looked beyond cut flowers to using driftwood and dried materials to reinvent bold topiary shapes for the home and for public spaces. The extraordinary vision of some of the country's top decorators has produced startling artworks in the forefront of British floristry and, some would say, at the cutting edge of modern sculpture, with creations that will sit as happily in an art gallery as in a contemporary home.

Flat pink heads of hydrangea, berried stems of cotoneaster and, below the shelf, buckets of lady's mantle (*Alchemilla mollis*), elevated from humble garden status to popular cut flower.

But one thing never changes. Flowers will always bring life to a room with their beauty and their fragrance. As Lady Pulbrook, ninety-three this year, says: 'I want everyone to enjoy flowers as much as I have. Flowers have the power to affect your attitude to life.'

The nectarine and curious peach,
Into my hands themselves do reach;
Stumbling on melons, as I pass,
Ensnared with flowers, I fall on grass.

Andrew Marvell, *The Garden*

classic visions

grand style

Planning is the key to creating flower arrangements for a special occasion. Visiting the location, taking note of the room's colour scheme, finding out how the table is to be set and who the guests will be – flowers for an all-male dinner will be very different to those for a mixed gathering – all have to be taken into account before even considering which flowers to use. At a formal gathering, many of the guests are likely to be strangers to each other, and a stunning arrangement can be a conversation piece guaranteed to break the ice.

Guests arriving for a formal dinner at Apsley House in London's Piccadilly are greeted by an exuberant mix of ornamental cherry blossom (*Prunus* 'Choshu-hizakura'), pink lilies and pale pink 'Anna' roses. Lime-green flower-heads of the guelder (*Viburnum opulus* 'Roseum') and *Euphorbia* introduce tones of acid green, and the whole is set against a backdrop of greenery provided by a variegated acer and a whitebeam (*Sorbus aria*). The arrangement gains extra drama from standing on a low pedestal in front of Canova's magnificent statue of Napoleon.

Loveliest of trees, the cherry now
Is hung with bloom along the bough.

A E Housman, *A Shropshire Lad*

The pink and gold colour scheme in the dining room at Apsley House in London was all-important in the choice of flowers for a formal dinner for thirty guests. Planning sessions revealed that the table was to be set with a gold damask cloth and a china service with green ivy leaves – more elements to be taken into account. Even the menu has to be discussed: a connoisseurs' dinner, for example, may well specify no scented flowers that would interfere with the bouquet of fine wines.

In this case, it was decided to echo the pink walls with a mix of lilies and rhododendrons in an even more intense shade, plus deep red fruit, accentuated by a dash of lime green. The display is such that the containers are hidden and hence unimportant, the flowers appearing to form an almost unbroken line through the centre of the table.

A long formal dinner table is innately grand and has such presence that there is no need to add displays of flowers to every corner of the room – they would simply compete for attention and unbalance the overall effect. A more understated treatment for a table featuring tall candelabra, as here, is to replace the central candle holder with a candle cup (see page 148) to hold trailing flowers that won't block the view across the table. Tiny pots of flowers for each lady's place setting can then be used to bring the eye down to table level.

Pink lilies, cherry blossom and rhododendrons repeat the colour theme of the display in the entrance hall. At the table they have been combined with red apples and red and green grapes, with further notes of green introduced by guelder (*Viburnum opulus* 'Roseum') and small sprays of spurge and hebe foliage. Sweet peas provide extra accents of pink, as do the very tips of young pieris shoots before they have faded to a standard green – an imaginative use of unusual material.

An equally formal dinner at the German ambassador's residence in Belgrave Square, London, illustrates a different approach to flowers for grand style. Here guests were shown into the blue drawing room with its handsome marble mantel and cream-silk upholstered chairs. The fireplace is the focal point of the room, further highlighted by an antique mirror reflecting a pretty chandelier; a group of flowers on the mantelpiece reinforces this effect. The single arrangement is designed to draw visitors into the room: too many flowers scattered seemingly at random can create confusion, as no one knows quite where to look. Keeping the arrangement at eye level is the most comfortable for guests who are standing, while the lower coffee table group takes into account that the guests will return to the drawing room after dinner for coffee.

A large arrangement such as this has to be put together in situ. To make it firm and rigid enough to be transported across town would automatically destroy the natural loose charm of the flowers. An arrangement the size of the one created for the entrance hall at Apsley House (page 36), for example, is impossible to move.

In an essentially pastel room the flowers emphasize the deep pink Aubusson rug – cerise amaryllis (*Hippeastrum*), semi-double camellias (*Camellia x williamsii* 'Donation') and azaleas, tempered by pale pink 'Anna' roses, jasmine (*Jasminum officinale*) and lilac (*Syringa vulgaris*). The compact coffee table grouping repeats the camellias and azaleas with anemones added.

They are not long, the days of wine and roses.

Ernest Dowson, *Vitae Summa Brevis*

The dining room at the embassy has walls painted in warm terracotta, a typical early nineteenth-century shade, and the apricot parrot tulips for the table decorations were chosen to harmonize with it. This was a men-only occasion and the containers form a strong element of the design, providing the opportunity to use more 'masculine' materials such as twine, cinnamon sticks and box. In contrast to the almost unbroken line of flowers on the table at Apsley House (page 38), these table arrangements are much smaller and hence more flexible. (They were pressed into service again the next day when lunch was served at a series of small tables.) Decorations such as these suffer no ill effects if made up the day before and kept in the cool room at the workshop for delivery straight to the table.

The dining room at the German Embassy in London is furnished with fine tapestries and a collection of sixteenth-century majolica plates on the chimneypiece. In such elegant surroundings the table has been set with a series of pots covered variously in box, rosemary and cinnamon sticks, tied in place with sisal and rope, and filled with apricot parrot tulips, alder catkins (*Alnus glutinosa*), copper beech leaves preserved with glycerine, ranunculus, guelder (*Viburnum opulus* 'Roseum') and the extraordinary green seed-pods of *Gomphorcarpus*.

weddings

Flowers are the most ephemeral yet most memorable elements of a wedding.

Their presence transforms the setting and creates a beautiful and fitting backdrop for

the bride. In a church the marriage service takes place at the chancel steps, the perfect

place to put an arrangement of flowers. The colour of the bride's and bridesmaids'

dresses, the architectural style of the church interior and, of course, the season will

all influence the choice of flowers. Above all, they should enhance the bride,

not upstage her.

Opposite: A truly classic arrangement in white and green that complements rather than competing with the stupendous stained glass windows at Holy Trinity, Sloane Street, London. Above: A scaled-down version is repeated at the back of the church.

I sing of brooks, of blossoms, birds, and bowers;
Of April, May, of June and July-flowers.
I sing of May-poles, Hock-carts, wassails, wakes,
Of bride-grooms, brides, and of their bridal-cakes.

Robert Herrick, *'The Argument of his Book', from Hesperides*

Holy Trinity on Sloane Street, London, is a church on a scale vast enough to dwarf all but the boldest arrangements of flowers. The classic white and green groups on either side of the chancel steps are enormous, which is vital if they are to have an impact on all that space. Two smaller and lower arrangements positioned at the beginning of the aisle, where guests arrive, help to focus attention on the nave and the chancel steps.

Such large and extravagant arrangements have to be done in situ. To avoid getting caught up in last-minute preparations on the day of the wedding, the flowers were arranged in the church the day before. As well as showing consideration for the bride and family, this also benefits the flowers, giving them time to 'settle' into position, while the cool church atmosphere preserves them at their peak.

Not all churches present such scope for decoration on a grand scale. In smaller buildings with room for just one group of flowers at the chancel steps, an alternative idea is to have a complementary arrangement for the altar. Another option is to decorate the pew ends – perhaps a simple ribbon motif leading to posies tied on the ends of the front two pews, or at most, flowers on alternate pew ends, but never on every one, which always looks overdone.

One of a pair of pedestals flanking the chancel steps at Sloane Street's Holy Trinity and decked with boughs of white cherry blossom (*Prunus*), white 'Pompeii' and 'Casa Blanca' lilies, loose yellowy-green bottlebrush heads of *Euphorbia characias wulfenii* and greeny-white pompoms of guelder (*Viburnum opulus* 'Roseum'), filled in with laurel and variegated ivy.

Despite good intentions, even the best-behaved bridesmaids seem prone to dangling their flowers from one finger or twirling them round and round, so giving each one a tied posy to carry makes perfect sense. It is the ideal shape for small hands to clasp easily, and binding the flower stems with tape not only creates a firm handle but also makes the posy robust enough to withstand a little rough handling without scattering petals everywhere. Another idea is to give the bridesmaids small flower-filled baskets to hold.

In the bridesmaid's posy, white ranunculus and double lisianthus (*Eustoma*) interwoven with spiky green hellebore seed-heads (*Helleborus foetidus*) echo the green and white theme of the main arrangements. Each flower has been individually arranged and then the stems tied and bound together with soft tape.

arrangements

Choosing the right flowers for a vase or container is a skill that takes years to acquire. Although colour schemes and personal taste are important, the overriding factor should be the season. Where possible, Pulbrook & Gould use only English-grown flowers – no tulips in summer or daffodils in autumn. Nothing beats the excitement of the first snowdrops of the year arriving in the shop.

Wherever practical, all arrangements are achieved by artful use of wire netting in water-filled containers. Using netting is essential for loose arrangements, while standing flowers directly in water means they 'drink' more readily than when placed in foam blocks.

A traditional cast-iron Warwick vase calls for a dramatic and important arrangement, here using spring flowers – lilac, amaryllis, camellia foliage, guelder (*Viburnum opulus* 'Roseum'), parrot tulips, hazel catkins (*Corylus avellana*), pussy willow (*Salix* spp.) and pink lilies.

*…as clear
As morning roses newly
washt with dew.*

Shakespeare, *The Taming of the Shrew*

Cream miniature roses with flowers
and foliage of variegated jasmine
and a few stems of humble spurge
exemplify an arrangement of flowers
that could easily have come straight
from the garden. This combination
smells heavenly and is ideal for a
feminine bedroom or small, intimate
sitting room.

Where was that cottage with its lilac trees,
Its windows wide, its garden drowsed with bees?

Mary Webb, *The Land Within*

The contrasting colours are surprisingly effective in this loose country arrangement for a desk or coffee table, where the lime-green of the tiny clusters of bupleurum flowers sharpens and offsets the sugar-pink ranunculus. The moulded grey Spanish pottery container is an integral part of the overall effect: as it is so charming, it shouldn't be overwhelmed by the flowers, and here the balance between the two is just right.

Ranunculus are popular cut flowers and their quality has been improved over the years as better varieties have been developed. British-grown ranunculus have a very short season, but anemones could easily be substituted in this arrangement.

A very simple classic arrangement using ranunculus, bupleurum and evergreen laurustinus (*Viburnum tinus*). A multitude of papery petals make up the dense round ranunculus flowers, which are members of the buttercup family, and their pink hue is echoed by the faint flush of pink on the laurustinus buds. Like lady's mantle (*Alchemilla mollis*), bupleurum is a useful yellowy-green-flowered species that adds a haze of colour to an arrangement. It has a rather attractive and unusual structure as its stems pass right through the leaves.

I remember, I remember
The roses red and white
The violets and the lily-cups,
Those flowers made of light.

Thomas Hood, *I Remember, I Remember*

So often the bathroom is completely overlooked when flowers are being arranged, but they should be just as essential as soft fluffy bath towels and fine soap. In this exquisitely simple arrangement for a bathroom wash-stand or dressing table, the flowers are definitely the most important element. No wire netting or artifice is involved, just short-stemmed roses loosely placed head-to-head in a small glass tank. It's an unwritten rule never to put a large vase of flowers in a bathroom: simplicity is all.

Keeping a small arrangement in glass looking fresh is easy, as the container can be gently tipped to one side to empty before adding fresh water.

Heads of 'Supreme' roses cut on short stems and at their flowering peak make an elegant addition to an antique silver dressing-table set. Cutting roses on a short stem will often extend the length of time that they last.

Come and see our new garland, so green and so gay:
'Tis the first fruits of spring and the glory of May.
Here are cowslips and daisies and hyacinths blue.
Here are buttercups bright and anemones too.

Traditional

When so much skill has been invested in an arrangement, it's only sensible to make the flowers work doubly hard. This informal group of hyacinths and anemones gracing a buffet table will sit equally well on a side table for a drinks party planned later in the week. Its low spreading shape is dictated by the glass vase's width and flared neck, with wire netting lending a helping hand.

There's a hidden art to trimming twiggy material like the catkins in this arrangement, which rarely come in a desirable shape but have to be judiciously pruned to suit the design – one false snip and it's spoiled.

Blue hyacinths and even deeper-toned anemones paired with yellowy-green guelder (*Viburnum opulus* 'Roseum') echo the colour scheme of the dining-room curtains. Catkins and berried ivy have been used to add interest, along with leathery bergenia leaves – another example of a fresh way of looking at an ordinary garden plant long taken for granted.

Summer afternoon – summer afternoon…the two most beautiful words in the English language.

Edith Wharton

A heavy-based cylindrical glass vase is a bold counterbalance to a big, loose arrangement, where a wintry framework of camellia foliage and catkins supports a selection of early spring flowers. Glass containers have become readily available in the past ten years or so, giving a far greater choice for arrangements; before that, it was nearly always the case that vases were china. As a general rule, glass containers tend to be simpler in style and altogether more contemporary. Here, using a glass cylinder for an essentially classical grouping of flowers gives it a contemporary slant, creating a more flexible arrangement that won't look out of place in either a traditional setting or a more modern room. With care, the underlying twiggy framework of this arrangement will outlast several changes of flowers. It should prove possible to refresh the arrangement by lifting it out all at once and holding it while someone else empties the vase. Refilling with fresh water will keep the flowers happy and the glass looking good.

Above: A classic early-spring arrangement of lilac, parrot tulips, guelder (*Viburnum opulus* 'Roseum') and oriental lilies with catkins and camellia foliage can be used with impunity in either a modern or a traditional setting. Opposite: White snapdragons (*Antirrhinum*), phlox and variegated weigela are more commonly seen in the garden but are reaching new heights of popularity as cut flowers. This arrangement also uses dill flowers (*Anethum graveolens*) from the herb garden: the flowers of dill are similar to those of cow parsley (*Anthriscus sylvestris*) but dill blooms in midsummer after cow parsley is finished. Also included are 'Bianca' roses, lisianthus (*Eustoma*) and 'Casa Blanca' lilies, whose sculptural green flower buds form part of the overall scheme.

christmas

Christmas just wouldn't be Christmas without holly, ivy, mistletoe and boughs of pine and larch, but every year, with a little imagination, new ways can be found to reinvent traditional decorations. Unusual materials play a part: dried globe artichoke heads and carved and dried grapefruit, for example, can be incorporated into more familiar designs to create something dramatically different. Varying your own approach to the home – one year focusing on a swag for the staircase, another on creating a display for the mantelpiece – can ring the changes each Christmas.

A splendidly seasonal swag made up at the workshop and delivered in time for Christmas. Every crab apple, lichened twig, spray of ivy berries and piece of pine and larch has been individually wired to a stout rope at the core of the swag. The weight is formidable and the swag must be firmly fixed, but once in place it will easily outlast the festivities.

At Christmas I no more desire a rose
Than wish a snow in May's new-fangled mirth;
But like of each thing that in season grows.

William Shakespeare, *Love's Labour's Lost*

A rustic open hearth is enhanced by a lavish yet very natural-looking swag, suitable for a country Christmas. The arrangement was built in situ, beginning with a frame of rolled wire netting firmly fixed to existing nails in the brickwork. Every piece is individually wired and attached to the frame and so closely packed that not so much as a hint of netting can be seen.

The greenery, of course, will gradually fade over the Christmas holiday but the dried ingredients – rolled bark, pine cones, grapefruit and artichoke heads – can be dismantled carefully and saved for another year. To dress up the swag for a more glittering occasion, all that's needed is to substitute coloured glass baubles for the dried grapefruit and artichoke heads.

A swag of variegated holly, blue pine, Japanese cedar (*Cryptomeria*) plus larch and golden yew (*Taxus baccata* 'Fastigiata Aureomarginata') greenery, studded with pine cones, dried globe artichoke heads, carved dried grapefruits and quills of rolled bark, all of which release a delicious scent in the warmth of the log fire. Whiskers of larch twigs are a typically innovative touch.

Heigh-ho! sing, heigh-ho! unto the green holly.

Shakespeare, *As You Like It*

A wreath on the front door is the time-honoured way to welcome visitors at Christmas. A big door is essential to carry off a wreath successfully, and the size and decoration of the wreath will depend on the style of the door, the position of the door knocker and letter plate, if any, and also on how ornate this hardware is.

Hanging a wreath can be a problem if there isn't a sturdy door knocker conveniently placed. With a heavy wreath such as the one pictured, it is safest to use a supporting wire running right over the top of the door and fastened inside. In this example, the wire is barely visible and is easily mistaken for part of the door panelling, but it could be disguised with ribbon.

On a simple cottage door, a plain bunch of pine and holly tied with ribbon is often more appropriate, and more in scale, than an elaborate wreath.

A simple wreath of blue pine and golden yew (*Taxus baccata* 'Fastigiata Aureomarginata'), with fresh apples and cones wired onto a moss frame. A scattering of mistletoe foliage and small sprays of alder cones and catkins (*Alnus glutinosa*) enhance the natural look.

Holly and ivy and mistletoe
Give me a red apple and let me go.

Traditional

A wreath should not only take into account the colour and style of the front door, as does this colourful wreath on a scarlet door, but should also set the tone for the decorations throughout the whole house. The theme can then be repeated at focal points throughout the building, in particular the staircase, mantelpiece and dining table. To add fresh flowers to a table decoration, traditional red roses or white hyacinths are ideal: long-lasting and undemanding, they complement Christmas greenery perfectly.

A contemporary version of the Christmas wreath mixes traditional greenery and cones with nuts, apples and pomegranates. The pomegranate slices have been lightly lacquered to keep them looking fresh. Neatly sawn Christmas logs are a witty addition. This heavy wreath is hung on a discreet wire taken up and over the door and securely fastened inside it. Wreaths for the front door are particularly long-lasting as they are not subjected to blasts of central heating or roaring log fires.

contemporary
visions

colour themes

In a contemporary setting, one strong colour is far more effective than a mixture of shades. Flowers are used for impact, almost for their shock value in an unexpected situation. They work best when used to create a pool of colour, repeating the hue of a cushion or a chair, echoing a patch of pigment on a painting and bringing the colour right into the room. Alternatively, they can be used to add a complete colour contrast. In a large space there may be room for more than one arrangement, but once the main grouping is in place, adding flowers in a different colour will dilute the impact and upset the focus. In most cases, strong dramatic blooms look best – amaryllis, lilies, tulips, all of which have graphically defined petals and outlines. This is not the time or the place for dainty frills or subtlety.

Many contemporary spaces are light-filled and white-painted, and, as white comes in many tints and tones, putting white flowers in a white room can have an interesting effect. Texture and shape become more important and the overall effect is much softer than using flowers of a contrasting colour. White on white suits a bedroom, for example, where serenity is paramount and startling colour contrasts less desirable.

A striking wall-sized painting by Alison Lambert dominates the space in a contemporary sitting room, dwarfing all around it. But this tall vase of lilies (*Lilium regale* 'Royal Gold') and crab apples (*Malus* 'Golden Hornet') has presence enough to hold its ground. Using yellow as a single colour brings warmth and light to an otherwise monochromatic scheme, though red amaryllis, too, would have sufficient impact to stand the contrast. The tall, narrow glass vase holds the flowers perfectly in place without recourse to wire netting or other props.

> *To gild refined gold, to paint the lily...*
> *Is wasteful and ridiculous excess.*
>
> Shakespeare, *King John*

Yellow is the lightest colour of all and the easiest to distinguish. There's no ambiguity as there is when blue shades into violet; no scope for debate over red versus scarlet. Yellow is an easy colour to incorporate into a room: cheerful and sunny by day; lambent, almost luminous as dusk falls; and undimmed by artificial light at night. The yellow lilies and golden crab apples in this room bring relief to a graphically stark painting and invite closer inspection. The sweet scent of the lilies draws the observer nearer, where the perfection of each petal and the almost crystalline structure of the underlying cells can be appreciated.

Lilies have been prized for thousands of years: they were grown by the ancient Egyptians and also by the Minoans nearly four thousand years ago. 'Royal Gold' is a hybrid of *Lilium regale*, a trumpet lily endemic to a small valley in China. In the wild, the flowers are white with a flush of yellow, which plant breeders have worked on over the years to produce trumpets of pure gold, which are at their best in July.

Using one undiluted colour for an arrangement – in this case a late-summer combination of lilies (*Lilium regale* 'Royal Gold') and crab apples (*Malus* 'Golden Hornet') – is the most dramatic and effective way to introduce flowers to a contemporary setting. A close look at the lily reveals that the stamens have been removed to stop the dark pollen from staining the petals or the furniture – or the clothes of anyone brushing past.

Bold yellow upholstery steals the scene in this room and demands a simple look that doesn't bring in another bright colour. Cream 'Maureen' tulips faintly flushed with gold echo the colour of the chairs while white Christmas roses (*Helleborus niger*) and anemones are suitably neutral. This ingenious arrangement uses three sizes of container, enabling tall and small flowers to be displayed together in a way they never could in a single vase. It also cleverly mimics the manner in which the flowers actually grow and is a valuable idea for spring, when so many species in flower are low-growing. A scattering of catkins in each vase unifies the theme.

Autumn fruits and foliage in shades of pink and red heighten the cool neutrality of walls faintly washed with a cream glaze. An enormous number of species has been plundered for this arrangement, including pink snow-berries (*Symphoricarpos*), sedum, spindle (*Euonymus europaeus*), red hypericum berries, blackberries, cotoneaster, stephanandra foliage and hydrangea heads. Laying a couple of hydrangeas on the table below stops the arrangement from looking static and enhances its natural, 'unarranged' effect. Adding a red apple or red grapes to the table would create the same impression.

Blue is an elusive and difficult colour to use in an arrangement. Blue flowers change all the time with the light, varying in intensity according to whether they are seen in daylight, candlelight or artificial light. At night they become duller, absorbing what light there is and fading to shades of grey or even black. No two blues are the same, from the intense true blue of a Himalayan poppy (*Meconopsis betonicifola*) to the inky violet of early spring irises (*Iris reticulata*). Early spring is the peak time for blues: irises, grape hyacinths (*Muscari*), hyacinths, anemones and scilla. The colour then reappears in midsummer with delphiniums, Himalayan poppies, salvias, campanulas and agapanthus lilies.

Blue was the obvious choice for an arrangement to complement a hall table used to display a collection of oriental blue and white ginger jars. Azure hyacinths were placed in a glass tank; leaving the bulbs and roots in place adds an extra dimension, creating a very natural look which is emphasized by a twiggy crown of dogwood.

Intense blue hyacinths were used to complement a display of blue and white antique ginger jars. Rather than using cut flowers, the bulbs and roots are still attached and each root system has been laboriously washed free of soil to avoid muddying the water. Dogwood (*Cornus*) twigs perform a double function: they support the top-heavy flowers and add extra height and depth to the arrangement. The twigs have been firmly bound to the external frame of twigs enclosing the glass tank for extra stability.

topiary

Historically, topiary is a gardening technique, a way of bringing structure and order to an otherwise soft and billowy mass of flowers. This is topiary in a new guise, reinvented as a permanent arrangement for interiors. The topiary designs on these pages owe more to the art of sculpture than to flower arranging and wouldn't look out of place in a modern art gallery.

New methods of arrangement allow the creation of traditional tightly clipped shapes with strong, bold outlines, or softer, more sinuous shapes. Thanks to modern advances in drying plant material, very little colour is lost. No longer do dried flowers come only in drab shades or garishly stained with artificial colour.

The first three topiary creations pictured here were photographed at Joseph's minimalist emporium on London's Sloane Avenue, where the sleek, modern interior throws the designs into sharp relief.

An illusory marjoram 'tree' with a driftwood 'trunk' is held in a wire pot of pebbles. The 'tree' is sculptural yet soft, with no hard lines but a richly textured canopy. Another bonus is that marjoram retains both its colour and its fragrance for a surprisingly long time.

Fruit white and lustrous as a pearl…
Lambent as the jewel of Ho, more strange
Than the saffron stone of Hsia.

Wang I, *The Lychee-tree*

These extraordinary obelisks look like relics of an ancient civilization and seem as far removed from conventional arrangements as a glass and steel tower is from a traditional thatched cottage. Made from dried lychees, each one individually wired by hand, the obelisks stand well over a metre (several feet) high and are a true labour of love. The rough patterned skins of the lychees are extremely tactile and few passers-by can resist stretching out a hand.

The warm, pinky-red tones of the lychees are the perfect foil for the display of lacquered Chinese pots in the background, all the more appropriate since the lychee is a Chinese fruit.

Thousands of dried lychees have been individually wired by hand before being attached to a framework to create a densely packed pyramid of pinky-brown hue. Each obelisk is set in a terracotta pot so thickly smothered with lichen moss as to resemble ancient stone.

O thou beauty both so ancient and so fresh.

St Augustine

An avant-garde sculpture of driftwood bleached to the colour of bone and interspersed with rings of lichen moss stands at the foot of the stairs at Joseph, London. Such an arresting piece acts as a signal, drawing people to it and so subliminally directing them towards the stairs. Works of art like this are ideal for offices, shops and reception areas, where they act as a focal point. They are also supremely practical, as they are unaffected by extremes of temperature, light and heat and do not require watering, though they might need dusting from time to time.

Discs of grey lichen moss tinged with black and layers of outlandishly shaped driftwood, buffed and bleached by the elements, have been sculpted into a surreal 'tree'. It stands in a classic white long-tom pot, enclosed by the sweep of a sinuous staircase.

A country dresser displaying a group of red amaryllis (*Hippeastrum*) and tulips flanked by a pair of topiary spirals shows how stylized arrangements can still sit quite comfortably with fresh flowers. The topiary spirals are formed from rolled wire netting twisted around a central wooden pole and then completely covered with lichen moss. The basket of fresh flowers holds not only red amaryllis and tulips, but also *Euphorbia*, holly berries stripped of their leaves, blue pine, photinia and skimmia. The basket has been lined with small birch logs that emphasize its informality, especially when combined with handfuls of nuts scattered on the dresser.

simplicity

At certain times of year, when a particular flower is at its peak, there can be no more breathtaking sight than a massed arrangement of a single species. A bowl brimming with roses spells luxury, extravagance, generosity of spirit. Yet it is also surprisingly practical: the flowers are easier to arrange as they are all roughly the same size and length, making light work of the design.

These massed arrangements are polar opposites to the huge mixed groups featured in the chapter 'classic visions', but they are just as impressive, and in some cases more so, as they focus attention solely on the form and colour of one single glorious flower.

Massed arrangements are bold and lavish, with maximum impact on their surroundings. In keeping with their contemporary settings, all the containers for these arrangements are deliberately simple – solid, heavy shapes in wood or glass.

A bowl of pink and red hydrangea heads causes the eye to focus on the individual florets to the exclusion of all else – there are no leaves or stems to create a distraction. Many hydrangea flowers change colour gradually with time, fading from magenta to pink to an elegant grey with only a hint of shell pink remaining.

Hydrangeas are notoriously temperamental as cut flowers, and there's a real skill to keeping them looking their best. This shallow wooden bowl is packed with wire netting to hold the near-spherical flower-heads in a gently rounded mass.

Three different varieties of rose have been used to build up this spectacular blaze of colour in an antique wooden bowl from Africa, juxtaposed against a contemporary red sofa. Using three distinct flower shapes in the same shade of red adds texture and interest to the overall design.

Blow like sweet roses in this summer air.

Shakespeare, *Love's Labour's Lost*

This arrangement is slightly more formal than those illustrated so far, as massed flowers for a table setting have to be a little more restrained. A densely packed vase of roses keeps the flowers well clear of the table, its tight arrangement making it unlikely that any flowers will trail or fall onto the dinner plates. Placing flowers head to head in this way is a technique that creates a satisfyingly solid arrangement with a strong outline, and roses respond to this treatment particularly well. Other flowers that can be similarly packed together include hydrangeas, ranunculus, anemones and parrot tulips, all of which have round, single flower-heads. Again, using flowers of just one colour creates the most dramatic effect.

Cream 'Mustique' roses in an opaque brown glass vase bring an element of tradition to a contemporary dining table set with rustic twiggy placemats and a Venetian-style candle holder. The backdrop is a large wall painting.

An arrangement that is not for the faint-hearted – and one that requires stout, thorn-proof gloves to create. Once again, the potential of a familiar material is revealed. Here, imaginative use has been made of the range of colours on blackberry stems, from purple-black ripe fruit through raspberry pink to under-ripe green, all set in a roughly hewn wooden bowl.

architectural influence

Just as the boundaries between fashion and interior design become blurred, with the same colours and fabrics defining what we wear, how we live and even what colours of flowers are in vogue, so too is architecture influential in deciding how flowers and plants should be used within a building.

Architecture today has come full circle, from the simplicity of Georgian designs through over-decorated Victorian follies to post-war utilitarian housing and finally back to a very simple modern style. Much contemporary design shows an American influence. The country was quick to embrace simple, uncluttered spaces such as lofts and warehouse conversions, which are now making their impact felt in Britain.

The house pictured belongs to Joseph Ettedgui, the driving force behind the eponymous men's and women's wear stores. The interior is characterized by strong lines and clarity of form, and an equally bold flower is needed if it is to make any kind of an impact. A *Phalaenopsis* orchid proves equal to the challenge. With its strong dark leaves and soaring stems of pure white flowers, it is an architectural plant in its own right. In this arrangement the vertical component has been exaggerated by a framework of tall dogwood stems.

A Chinese grain basket planted with *Phalaenopsis* for a streamlined modern look. Burgundy stems of dogwood (*Cornus*) give extra support to the flowering stems and add an element of structure for an even more graphic effect.

...a whiter shade of pale.

Keith Reid

In an all-white room with neutral upholstery, strong colour can be intrusive and even irritating. Instead, pure white flowers and berries are the best option: they can be appreciated for their simplicity and beauty, not just because their colour shrieks loudly. Every aspect of this sitting room is spare and uncluttered, from the strong lines of the fireplace to the simple curves of the armchairs and the statue, emphasizing the economy of form and the restriction of superfluous detail.

Other white flowers that would suit such a setting include the pure linear form of sculptural white arum lilies (*Zantedeschia aethiopica*) or tall white foxgloves (*Digitalis*).

A mass of heavily fruited snowberries (*Symphoricarpos*) softens an uncompromisingly graphic contemporary sculpture. The stems are held in a glass tank filled with a mixture of small stones and seashells and supported by a cradle of driftwood. On the lower table is a vase of simple white Amazon lilies (*Eucharis amazonica*), proving that an absence of colour can still be stylish. The lilies flower from early summer right through to winter, while snowberries are available from late summer.

An altogether more skeletal arrangement: a
many-branched piece of driftwood set in a
glass tank weighted with pitted, weathered
pebbles and a layer of tiny seashells almost
as fine as sand. A lamp behind it adds drama,
highlighting its bare, wintry outline – the
ultimate in minimalist chic.

For under thorn and bramble
About the hollow ground
The primroses are found.

A E Housman, *The Lent Lily*

Architectural influence isn't confined to contemporary designs. The Georgians, who pioneered simple, symmetrical Italianate style, were the modernists of their era and had firm ideas on the use of colour and decoration. In this room with its painted panelling, any colour stronger than these pale primroses would be strident and attention-seeking. Placing them at the foot of a delicate antique sculpture gently draws attention to it without obscuring it in any way. A shallow bowl of pale Christmas roses or snowdrops would look equally complementary.

A wooden bowl planted with humble spring primroses (*Primula vulgaris*) offsets a finely detailed bust in a typical panelled Georgian drawing room, highlighting the sculpture without overwhelming it. Although primroses are available in a palette of bright colours, the unimproved original has to be the best in this situation. Using plants rather than fresh flowers guarantees a much longer-lasting arrangement.

country
visions

first impressions

The front door and entrance hall provide the first glimpse of a home. As they create a lasting impression that sets the tone for the whole house, it is worth taking the time and trouble to have some appropriate flowers in place. Except on very special occasions, this is no place to set an over-elaborate arrangement; simplicity creates the best impression, as this unsophisticated autumn wreath proves. Pine cones, bare twigs and fruits are subtly seasonal, and their understated colours don't overwhelm the plain wooden and glass door.

On a gloomy autumn day the sight of a cheerful light shining through a decorative wreath is a welcoming sight. In this instance, it also has an extremely practical function, acting as a reminder that there is solid glass behind it.

A simple country wreath adds charm to a cottage door and enlivens a stark entrance. Larch, pomegranates and various pine cones have been mixed with driftwood and the bare red branches of manzanita (*Arctostaphylos manzanita*) to create a rustic arrangement. As it is hanging on a glass door, the wreath must be completely mossed at the back to hide the mechanics of the arrangement.

Annihilating all that's made
To a green thought in a green shade.

Andrew Marvell, *The Garden*

This well-used country porch is a practical storeroom for riding boots and equipment, but the desk used as a hall table is still deserving of decoration. Delicate flowers would look out of place here – greenery is all it needs to add a welcoming touch, in this case fennel (*Foeniculum vulgare*) and *Gomphorcarpus*.

Until recently fennel would not have formed part of a flower arrangement. As a herb it was considered fit only for the kitchen or the herb garden. But its graceful, feathery leaves are in fine fettle from early summer to late autumn, and the flower-heads are a natural substitute for its near relative cow parsley (*Anthriscus sylvestris*), which has a short flowering season.

As this is a no-nonsense, workaday sort of place, an unassuming antique wooden milk bucket from Africa has been used to hold the arrangement. It's a good example of how bright flowers aren't always necessary – after all, as the British garden designer Gertrude Jekyll once pointed out, green is a colour.

In an antique bucket, stems of feathery fennel have been combined with the fine linear leaves and green seed-heads of *Gomphorcarpus*, a native North American plant. Once popular for its flowers, it is now rapidly gaining attention for its papery, green seed-pods with their light furring of bristles.

garden flowers

In a perfect world a bunch of flowers for the house would be picked from the garden and brought straight to the table. In practice, it's not so simple. The day that roses are needed for an arrangement is inevitably the day that mildew has blighted them. But there is a way to compromise, by gathering garden foliage, flowers and berries, and then buying extra flowers to add colour and form. Choosing additional flowers carefully so that they blend in will result in an arrangement that really does look as though it has all come from the garden.

The vase pictured is filled with standard garden stalwarts such as hebe, abelia and blackberries, but supplements them with commercially grown 'Doris Ryker' spray roses, which look every bit as delicate and unassuming as their garden-grown counterparts. A large-flowered or modern rose would not have the same effect and would spoil the naïve charm of the other flowers.

Abelia x *grandiflora*, with its small pink flowers encircled by pink-tinged sepals is a familiar garden plant, along with hebe and, at a pinch, hedgerow blackberries. Adding sprays of the coral-pink rose 'Doris Ryker' completes the garden look without giving anyone cause to suspect that the roses aren't home-grown. Furry grey leaves of *Lotus hirsutus* complete the picture.

Old garden roses have such a short season that cunning is called for to have them in the house all summer long. Commercial 'Anna' roses are softened by the addition of delicate umbels of fennel flowers (*Foeniculum vulgare*) from the herb garden. Contrasting evergreen camellia foliage with red photinia leaves is another trick that suggests a simple bunch of country flowers.

He promised he'd bring me a basket of posies,
A garland of lilies, a garland of roses.

Traditional

The impression given by a glorious basket of blooms is that they have been cut from a herbaceous border overflowing with summer flowers. But going out to the garden, scissors in hand, there is every chance that the roses will have greenfly or the lilies will be spoiled with rain spots. Garden flowers grown for the cut-flower market are raised in protected conditions and so are nearer perfection than most gardeners could ever achieve. Also, vagaries of sun and shade within a garden often mean that plants that should be in flower at the same time quite often aren't: buying an arrangement of country flowers guarantees that everything is as nature intended – only better.

A high-summer symphony in blue and pink composed of blue delphiniums and lisianthus (*Eustoma*), pink hydrangeas, lavatera and phlox, with bold 'Orlando' lilies and small-flowered pink abelia, set in a basket woven from olive twigs. The basket has a liner and the arrangement depends on a base of wire netting for stability.

The reds, pinks and magentas I mix fearlessly and, if I possessed one, I should put them in a chalice of brilliant hard green malachite.

Constance Spry

The low, densely packed group of flowers pictured here contains only well-known garden species, including a fair proportion of shrubs. To some gardeners it may seem shocking that shrubs have been lopped simply to adorn a table, but others will recognize that 'picking to prune' is not such a bad thing. By taking out a straggling branch here, an overlapping one there, the overall shape of the bush can be improved while providing useful foliage and blossom in season for the house.

The arrangement relies on some of the commonest shrubs: escallonia, here used for its foliage only; weigela, whose pretty pink bells are found in nearly every garden in spring; and a heavily berried prickly relative of heather, *Gaultheria mucronata*. 'The Fairy', a polyantha rose bearing sprays of small pink flowers, is both a garden variety and a commercially grown one, so its inclusion is doubly apposite.

Tucked in among the more visible bright pink berries of *Gaultheria mucronata* and sprays of 'The Fairy' pink roses are deep pink penstemons and pink weigela, with every available gap filled with the glaucous leaves of rue (*Ruta graveolens*), neat dark green escallonia foliage and trails of soft grey ballota. The arrangement was made using wire netting in a low earthenware dish and would suit a coffee table or a side table.

Harebells, a thousand harebells to ring at dawn just as the cock starts crowing…

Colette

Certain containers have a simplified country air about them. Jugs are almost always emphatically rustic, and a rotund humble jug makes an informal arrangement much easier to achieve than trying to use a linear, overly elegant glass vase. Easily come by in junk shops and flea markets, jugs need not be in pristine condition, as a mass of flowers will hide any imperfections. A plastic liner can even reprieve a cracked specimen. This arrangement depends on a plain blue and white jug for its simple charm, the colour echoed in the selection of flowers, which range from blue-eyed borage from the herb garden to the slightly sinister hooded flowers of monkshood.

An arrangement of cottage-garden favourites includes monkshood (Aconitum), scabious, borage (*Borago officinalis*), hydrangea, penstemon, phlox and myrtle (*Myrtus*), with complementary shades of grey from narrow-leaved *Helichrysum italicum* foliage and green-grey poppy seed-heads, all standing in a pretty country jug.

And on that bed a basket –
A basket of sweet flowers.

Anonymous, *The Key of the Kingdom*

A country arrangement is intrinsically informal and, to be successful, should look as though it was entirely determined by what flowers were waiting to be picked from the garden. None of the arrangements in this section feature any form of structure or symmetry: they appear just to have happened. This is partly due to the sheer numbers of different flowers in each one – sometimes just one stem, at most two or three of one species – implying that this was all that was in flower in the borders that day.

This glass tank holds a great variety of flowers, and the closer you look, the more detail is revealed, from sprigs of rosemary and rue picked for their foliage, to tiny white myrtle flowers and lemon geranium leaves.

A delicate and charming white arrangement for a bathroom or dressing table is filled with jasmine (*Jasminum officinale*), dill (*Anethum graveolens*), phlox, lisianthus (*Eustoma*), myrtle (*Myrtus*), the starry flowers of the potato vine (*Solanum jasminoides* 'Album') and foliage from rosemary, rue (*Ruta graveolens*), hebe and scented geraniums (*Pelargonium crispum*).

plants

Planted containers are invaluable in winter when seasonal cut flowers become more expensive. With regular watering and misting, rooted plants are able to tolerate central heating far better than cut flowers, making them longer-lasting and so better value at this time of year. In fact, heat can be a positive advantage and used to bring on flowers ahead of their season, as in the best country house tradition when plants in the greenhouse were coaxed into early bloom for the mistress of the manor. A favourite container can be used to hold plants that are already potted up, making it easier to change the display regularly – a layer of moss will disguise ugly plastic plant pots. Plants are easier to give than cut flowers. They don't need immediate attention, making them an ideal gift for a friend in hospital, for example. And a basket of snowdrops (*Galanthus*) or daffodils (*Narcissus*) makes a doubly useful present for a gardener, as the bulbs can be planted in the garden when the arrangement has faded.

Scientific developments have made orchids into affordable plants for the house. Where it once took upwards of seven years to raise an orchid from seed to flowering plant, cloning techniques have greatly reduced the wait for flowers. Their exotic native habitat means that orchids thrive in central heating and make tolerant house plants that need watering just once a week. *Oncidium obryzatum* 'Little Angel' is an imposing plant that sends out sprays of flowers 60 centimetres (2 feet) long, here enhanced with supporting dogwood (*Cornus*) stems. The striking container is a wire basket filled with empty terracotta pots to hide the inner plastic pot.

Wintry white arrangements like the two pictured are very welcome when the garden is at its bleakest and flowers are hard to come by. A low basket crammed with Christmas roses makes an ideal focal point for a side table in a sitting room, while a pot of exuberant jasmine will bring life and light, not to mention fragrance, to the home. As it is so highly scented, it should be placed in an entrance hall or large, open-plan room so that its fragrance can permeate every corner. Since the jasmine is the same species as the common garden climber, it can be planted out in spring if given time to acclimatize to normal temperatures after the protection of being grown indoors.

Above: Christmas roses (*Helleborus niger*) are garden plants that can be put into a shady spot in the garden and relied upon to come up year after year. This mesh basket has been lined with moss and planted up with hellebores grown under glass so that no wintry mud splashes have spoiled their pure white petals. Opposite: A basket of jasmine (*Jasminum officinalis*) forced into flower out of season is a rare treat. The buds have a tendency to dry out in centrally heated houses so the plant should be kept well watered and misted daily, but provided this is done, it should transplant to the garden without fuss once it has finished flowering.

You see, I will not hear a word spoken against my snowdrops. They are heavenly, when they are out, and set in a glass bowl, so that their fresh green stalks are seen with the water bubbles glistening around them.

Beverley Nicholls, *Down the Garden Path*

Snowdrops are among the first flowers of spring and a sight to gladden the heart. By growing them in a cold greenhouse, these snowdrops have been coaxed into flower early. The protection of the glass roof has ensured that each petal is perfect – not splashed with mud, bowed with frost or tattered by slugs. The snowdrops were grown in pots and then planted into a lined basket and generously blanketed with moss. Kept on a table in a cool room, they should last for several weeks.

A basket of woven grass lined with moss holds a clump of snowdrops (*Galanthus spp.*) that will happily transfer to the garden when they have finished flowering. In fact, planting them 'in the green', when the flowers have faded but the leaves are still fresh, gives them a much better chance of survival than planting dry bare bulbs in the autumn.

candles

Candlelight is gentle and romantic and just as flattering to flowers as it is to faces. Adding candles to a table arrangement brings extra focus to the flowers and softens harsh colours, as well as adding to the atmosphere at dinner.

The easiest way to make a table arrangement is to use a pad of florists' foam with a waterproof backing: a decorative container is unnecessary as it will be entirely hidden by flowers. Candles can be fixed straight into florists' foam and layers of flowers built up around them; it also keeps the arrangement low – vital if conversation is to take place across it. Scented candles shouldn't be used for the dinner table but can be a nice touch for a hall table or sitting room.

Never risk leaving lighted candles unattended: imperfections in the wax can cause a candle to burn too quickly and flare up unexpectedly.

Deep autumn red is the theme for this striking arrangement featuring red nerines, crab apples, red roses and lilies, with red photinia foliage and contrasting green-berried ivy, centred on a group of thick, slow-burning church candles.

This contemporary arrangement is suitable for a side table rather than a dinner table as it has been made in a deep-sided wooden bowl. The bowl holds a pad of florists' foam for a base, to which has been added an asymmetrical grouping of pale honey-coloured candles surrounded by variegated holly (*Ilex* spp.), pine cones, fresh apples and apricot arum lilies against a ruff of pine and twigs of manzanita (*Arctostaphylos manzanita*).

He hangs in shades the orange bright,
Like golden lamps in a green night.

Andrew Marvell, *Bermudas*

Changing the shape of the candles has a marked effect on the arrangement, the hard angular lines making this whole grouping more suitable for a contemporary interior. Candlelight might seem the complete antithesis of modern living, but a high-tech setting and an age-old form of lighting make a pleasing contrast. The irregular outline of candles of differing heights is complemented by an encircling base of foliage and seed-heads. Although the seed-heads are on the point of drying, their pale green colour gives a fresh effect. A more autumnal centrepiece could be created using the same principles but replacing the seed-heads with similarly shaped walnuts or even poppy seed-heads.

This minimalist arrangement uses square candles for graphic effect and has a simple base of golden yew (*Taxus baccata* 'Fastigiata Aureomarginata'), rue (*Ruta graveolens*) and fuzzy green seed-heads of *Gomphorcarpus*.

Although this is essentially a winter arrangement, it gives a hint of how candles needn't be confined to long dark evenings. This simple silver dish would look just as good filled with summer flowers – roses or lisianthus – for a dinner party; while for dining al fresco, flowers could be grouped around the base of a plain glass storm lantern.

In a formal setting, candelabra can be used to hold flowers as well as candles by replacing one of the candles with a candle cup – a small reservoir of wet Oasis that can be filled with tiny flowers or trailing stems.

Aromatic eucalyptus gum nuts, lemon thyme (*Thymus x citriodorus*), rue (*Ruta graveolens*) and juniper (*Juniperus* spp.) complement a lightly scented candle set in a silver dish and surrounded with white anemones and small cones brushed with the merest hint of silver. As the candle is scented, this particular arrangement is better suited to a sitting room than to the dinner table.

the country bunch

The country bunch is quintessentially English: a natural, informal, loosely tied bunch of flowers that immediately evokes images of picnics, lanes edged with cow parsley, the loveliest of long hot days, opera in the open air. In years gone by, the flowers came straight to the shop from suppliers' gardens, ready tied in the prettiest of posies. These days, they are done in the shop, but the bunches of flowers retain a simple charm that just can't be faked. Any combination of country flowers and foliage can be used – even a handful of aromatics from the herb garden will do, as long as the flowers fit the occasion.

Flowers for a picnic: daisy-like feverfew (*Tanacetum parthenium*), which grows as freely as a weed in sunny gardens, cow parsley (*Anthriscus sylvestris*) straight from the hedgerow, mixed with sugar-pink flowers of lavatera, one of the most vigorous of shrubs, and pink and white hydrangeas.

Kitchen Kilner jars filled with flowers such as a child might gather: white snapdragons (*Antirrhinum*) with open yellow heads of fennel (*Foeniculum vulgare*); yellow daisies; plus a jar of lady's mantle (*Alchemilla mollis*) and cow parsley (*Anthriscus sylvestris*).

Bring baskets now, and sally
Upon the spring's array,
And bear from hill and valley
The daffodil away
That dies on Easter day.

A E Housman, *The Lent Lily*

Even the most familiar spring flowers can shine with special treatment. Massing flowers together gives a sense of extravagance, and a vase brimming with daffodils in early spring makes a wonderful arrangement for a sitting room. The simplest varieties of daffodils are best, as extra colours will only detract from their initial impact. On a practical note, with such a vast number of flowers in one vase, the water will need topping up daily.

Daffodils are the essence of spring and are at their best massed together and unadorned except for a few catkins. Packed into a glass vase, their heads form a cloud of purest yellow, reflecting and strengthening the yellow walls of the room and casting a pool of colour onto the table.

The success of the country bunch depends on mimicking flowers freshly gathered from the garden or hedgerow, using just a few choice flowers of each sort garlanded with familiar greenery. This bunch makes use of hitherto overlooked shrubs, which will be mostly evergreens in spring as many deciduous species have yet to put out leaves. Their perennially useful green leaves have often been underrated; especially neglected is ivy, which has decorative berries all through winter. Here the shrubs' foliage has been mixed with the earliest spring flowers – sweetly scented hyacinths, miniature narcissi and almond blossom.

A bunch of country flowers lies on a hall table waiting to be set in a jug. Evergreen garden foliage includes skimmia, pieris, berried ivy and laurustinus (*Viburnum tinus*), supplemented with birch catkins (*Betula*) to make a perfect foil for early almond blossom (*Prunus dulcis*) and creamy hyacinths. Other flowers studded throughout the bunch include ranunculus, 'Tête-à-Tête' miniature daffodils, the yellow sweet-pea-like flowers of *Coronilla valentina glauca* 'Citrina' and pink-flushed Christmas roses (*Helleborus niger*). Pictured above is the same bunch but with a few snowdrops added to change the emphasis very subtly.

the workshop

a country garland

1 A circlet of flowers makes a charming traditional bridesmaid's headdress. All the flowers and foliage to form the circlet must be individually wired. Some of the flowers are even broken down into their constituent florets before wiring, a process known as pipping. Then the wired stems are bound with soft green tape so that no sharp ends can scratch hands or head.

2 The base of the circlet is a length of strong hat wire shaped into a circle the exact size of the bridesmaid's head. The wired foliage and flowers – rosemary and ivy leaves, lavender, 'The Fairy' roses and the soft furry calyces of ballota – are laid in place on the hat wire and bound on with fine silver wire. The excess wire from the wired stems is then cut off, to keep the circlet as light as possible.

3 Choosing small flowers ensures the circlet is light and easy to wear, and the rosemary, lavender and roses will also make it deliciously scented. The circlet can be made up the day before it is needed, then kept damp and cool to preserve the flowers. A posy of matching flowers is tied with ribbon.

malmaison rose

1 The malmaison rose was perfected by Constance Spry and based on an earlier, Victorian tradition – creating an overblown rose from the petals of many perfect roses. The petals are wired together to make one splendid flower. All the rage in the 1940s and '50s, malmaison roses were made regularly for ladies attending society balls. One would be tucked into a waistband, attached to a fold at the back of a dress or pinned to a clutch bag. The name probably comes from the large cabbage roses grown by Empress Josephine in her famous rose garden at the Château de Malmaison. The many hours and very special talent needed to perfect a malmaison rose make it a dying art, nurtured now only by a few people. Such a rose might be ordered today for a bride's posy.

2 The petals are stripped from countless roses, and hundreds are discarded because they are too small or have the tiniest imperfection. Those that make the grade are each individually pinched and folded to retain their natural shape and pierced with a fine wire, which is then pinched together to secure it. Hot hands will spoil the petals, so the wiring has to be done in shifts. Once the petals have been wired, the malmaison rose is made up in the shape of a real rose. A perfect rosebud forms the centre, then, working outwards, petal upon petal is added, and the wires twisted to form a thick stem.

3 Eventually a border of real rose leaves is added. Victorian examples might have used concentric rings of different-coloured petals, completed with a row of glossy camellia leaves or a paper lace frill. Finally, the stem is bound and tied with silk ribbon and the rose is ready for the bride. It is one of the most ephemeral of arrangements, lasting just for one special day. Because of the skill involved it is the sort of commission few people undertake, and the ability to make a malmaison rose is fast becoming a lost art.

container flowers

1

A container such as this rustic bark basket needs a plastic liner to make it watertight. Wire netting, crumpled into a ball and pushed firmly into the liner, is used to hold the flowers in place. To stop the ball of netting from slipping, it is secured with reel wire threaded through the netting and wrapped right around the outside of the plastic liner. As an extra precaution more reel wire is pushed through the rim of the basket and looped over to hold the liner and netting firmly in place.

2

The liner is filled with water and the shape of the arrangement established with berried ivy and rosemary. Foliage always goes in first to form the basic structure from which to work, and to cover up the netting. Then guelder, bupleurum and *Gomphorcarpus* seed-pods are added to strengthen the outline. Turning the basket as it is filled avoids a lopsided finished result.

3

Next, the flowers are incorporated, again turning the basket as they are added. Hyacinths, parrot tulips and ranunculus are clustered together rather than dotted sporadically through the arrangement; the hyacinths go in first, then the tulips and lastly the ranunculus. Because the latter have the smallest flowers, they are useful for filling small gaps. The overall aim is to achieve a natural look and one that is not overly symmetrical.

Fresh garden herbs are the mainstay of the posy shown on the left. A border of glaucous rue (*Ruta graveolens*) leaves and dill flowers (*Anethum graveolens*), a close relative of ever-popular cow parsley (*Anthriscus sylvestris*), surrounds a cluster of old-fashioned roses with creamy white petals. The stems have been bound with a sheath of tightly wound greeny-grey ribbon that cleverly echoes the tone of the rue leaves, and finished by a double twist of green and gold 'string ribbon'. As with the arrangement below, these bunches are designed to be clasped in the hands.

tying posies

Pictured right is one of the simplest of all raffia-tied posies: a handful of 'mixed greens' including all sorts of foliage hitherto overlooked – grasses, fresh mint (*Mentha* spp.), greeny-grey rue leaves (*Ruta graveolens*) and sprays of hypericum berries that have yet to turn their characteristic shade of red. Added to these are shyly subtle lady's mantle (*Alchemilla mollis*), bupleurum and some unassuming sprigs of dill flowers (*Anethum graveolens*), all tied in a loose natural bunch.

The extremely modern arrangement on the left couldn't present a greater contrast to the posies opposite. The arum lilies are unusual in that they are much smaller than those commonly seen for sale. They have been arranged so that the elegant fine tips of the flowers radiate outwards, and then tied just below the flower-heads with a satin ribbon fastened with a button. Such an arrangement demands that the flowers be carried in a completely different manner, held across the arm. Although this is contemporary in presentation, there is a retrospective influence at work here, too, as arum lilies feature heavily in designs from the Art Nouveau era.

On the right, a new twist on an old favourite uses masses of fresh, rather than dried, lavender to create a headily fragrant posy. Varying the length of the stems produces the domed effect, while binding the flowers tightly behind the heads forms the stalks into a complementary fan. Ribbon woven from natural jute and backed with moss makes a rustic but pretty finishing touch. The lavender 'Hidcote Blue' was used for its singular intensity of colour.

Various gauges of wire, as shown on the left, are needed for different jobs. When flowers such as hyacinths, for example, have been 'pipped' – or broken down into their constituent florets – the finest rustproof silver stub wires are used to wire the individual florets. They are also used for wiring rose petals and lily of the valley, and for making up circlets for bridesmaids. Stronger stub wires are used for supplementing the stems of heavier flowers or creating stems for items like walnuts or dried oranges. Black reel wire is heavy-duty gauge for use where it won't be seen, while green plastic-coated wire is extra proof against rusting and scratching. Silver reel wire is ideal for use with glass containers, as it reflects the light and becomes almost invisible. Various widths of soft Oasis tape are used to fix Oasis to containers and trays or to fasten netting to a glass vase, while pale green gutter tape is used to cover wires for fine work such as circlets or brides' posies.

equipment

Galvanized wire netting, pictured right, with a 5cm (2in) mesh is essential for nearly all flower arrangements and for constructing topiaries, swags and arches. When netting is used in an arrangement, it allows flowers to stand in water, by far the most natural way of keeping them. Scissors are largely a matter of personal choice – every florist has a favourite pair, though some prefer to use a knife. In general, the bigger scissors are the sharpest and have more leverage, though in really tough cases, secateurs are invaluable.

Oasis, a water-retaining foam that holds flowers firmly in position, comes in many shapes and sizes, some of which are shown on the left. Rings and pads with ready-made plastic bases are ideal for table decorations and mean that no container is necessary as the Oasis will be entirely concealed by flowers. Large blocks can easily be cut to size, from a tiny cylinder to fit the smallest candle cup to a shape custom-made to hold a heavy candle arrangement completely steady. Oasis is a replacement material for arrangements where moss would traditionally have been used and it is much more practical and a lot easier to handle.

Country bunches and traditional posies look much more authentic tied with simple natural materials (pictured right) such as raffia, a fibre woven from palm leaves or 'rope' twisted from fibrous coconut husks. Sisal and rush yield useful twines and strings, too, and the heavier types can be used to decorate containers for a rustic look.

Moss, shown left, is masterful at disguising the more prosaic elements of an arrangement, as well as being decorative in its own right. It makes the perfect lining for an openwork basket or a glass dish to be filled with pots, it provides the perfect soft backing for door wreaths and it can be glued onto a frame to create a piece of topiary.

accessories

Boxes of dried lavender, pictured right, arrive with the flowers tied in bunches ready for use. 'Hidcote Blue' is the favourite variety, for its intense colour that survives the drying process undimmed. Dried lavender has many uses: to decorate or to mix into dried arrangements – especially sculptural topiaries – or to wire into garlands and swags.

Cones, shown on the left, are yet more festive features, wired into swags and wreaths, garlands and table decorations, or gilded and wired into pretty Christmas tree decorations. Many different varieties are used, from tiny alder cones to familiar pine cones.

Nuts and spices, pictured right, are accessories for autumn and Christmas, when they are wired and added to wreaths, swags and table decorations. Individual nuts and cinnamon sticks can be wired and used to decorate the Christmas tree, while cloves are an essential component of traditional pomanders, in which they are used to spike oranges which are then dried slowly.

Old terracotta pots, pictured left, are far superior to plastic any day but they have many uses beyond simply holding soil and plants. The smaller ones can be strung into an unusual garland or wired and added to wreaths and swags for a decorative touch. On page 136, for example, small pots have been used to fill a large wire basket and hide the plastic container within.

containers

Jugs and pretty containers such as those on the right complement an arrangement and give flowers a more natural appearance, especially in a country house or a cottage bedroom. Where the flowers are simple – just a few roses or stems of garden flowers like phlox or peonies – then the jug becomes an important part of the arrangement. It is well worth building up a collection from junk shops and market stalls.

Dramatic antiques like the Warwick vases and metal goblets pictured left are treasured containers and used for inspirational displays in Pulbrook & Gould's premises. Their presence and dignity add weight and emphasis to an arrangement. The Warwick vases are copies of an urn excavated in the eighteenth century, and similar items sometimes turn up at auction or in antiques shops. A scattering of pebbles can be used to add weight and stability to a glass vase or to cover the surface of a potted plant.

Today glass vases such as those shown on the right seem to be more popular than ceramic ones. Glass comes in a huge range of shapes and sizes suitable for traditional or contemporary interiors. As well as being sleek and attractive, it is eminently practical, as it shows at a glance when water levels are low.

index

Figures in italics refer to photograph captions

acknowledgements

Many people in many different ways have assisted in the production of this book. It would be difficult to acknowledge everyone, but we wish to express sincere thanks to everyone who allowed cameras and lights to invade their houses, or worked unreasonable hours without complaint, particularly to David Montgomery for his patience and attention to detail.

John Byrom Design Ltd
Mrs Thorpe
Mrs Janie Schaffer
Mrs Martine Montgomery
Holy Trinity Church, Sloane Street, London SW1
Apsley House
Mr and Mrs Joseph Ettedgui
Joseph Men's Store, Sloane Avenue, London SW3

Snapdragon, Fulham Road, London SW3
Oggetti, Fulham Road, London SW3
Fleur Rossdale, interior design consultant
Charlton House and The Mulberry Restaurant, Shepton Mallet, Somerset
Harald Altmaier
Embassy of the Federal Republic of Germany, Belgrave Square, London SW1
Mrs Sally Green
Miss Beryl Larken

Special thanks go to all the staff, both past and present, who throughout the years have given their energy, enthusiasm, support and loyalty combined with extraordinary talent, making the success possible.